SC SHORE CONSULTING

ABOUT THE AUTHOR

Jeff Shore is a highly sought-after sales keynote speaker, author and consultant. For more than three decades, Jeff has guided sales executives and sales teams in large and small companies across the globe to deliver profitable customer-first sales results.

In a crowded field of sales keynote speakers and sales training programs, Jeff Shore stands out with his research-based "buying formula" methodology. Combining his extensive front-line sales experience with the latest leading-edge research into buyer psychology, Jeff has created a highly effective, personalized way to reset sales paradigms and deliver industry-leading results.

Jeff holds the prestigious Certified Speaking Professional designation from the National Speakers Association (NSA) and is a member of the NSA's exclusive Million Dollar Speaker's Group. Jeff tailors every keynote to your business and your team while electrifying your audience through captivating real-world case studies, inspiring personal stories, hard-working and straightforward sales strategies, and his engaging trademark humor.

Jeff won't just teach you how to sell…he'll show you how to change your mindset AND how to change your world.

jeffshore.com
jeff@jeffshore.com
(844) 54-SHORE

Handling Sales Objections

8 Reality-Based Techniques for Tackling Tough Objections

BY JEFF SHORE

ISBN: 978-0-9884915-3-3

Copyright 2017 by Jeff Shore and Shore Consulting, Inc.

All rights reserved. Printed in the United States of America. Except as permitted under the United States Copyright Act of 1976, no part of this publication may be reproduced or distributed in any form or by any means, or stored in a database or retrieval system, without the prior written permission of the publisher.

Cover design by Kista Cook

Shore Consulting books are available at special quantity discounts to use as premiums and sales promotions or for use in corporate training programs. To contact a representative, please visit the Contact page at www.jeffshore.com or call +1 844-54-SHORE.

CONTENTS

Introduction IX

Chapter 1: *Embrace the Objection* 3

Chapter 2: *The Reality of Compromise* 11

Chapter 3: *Three Reality-Embracing Questions* 19

Chapter 4: *The Law of Social Proof* 27

Chapter 5: *Transfer of Ownership* 35

Chapter 6: *Can You Live With It?* 43

Chapter 7: *He Likes It...She Doesn't* 51

Chapter 8: *We Need To Think About It* 59

VIII   HANDLING SALES OBJECTIONS

INTRODUCTION

If you've been in sales for any length of time, you have faced sales objections. Small or big. Real or imagined. Easy or tough.

Sales objections are as predictable and consistent as the sunrise.

Unfortunately, many salespeople see sales objections as an early warning sign that the sale is about to self-destruct. And just the thought of handling tough sales objections is sometimes enough to trigger that sinking feeling in your stomach.

However, here's the truth: objections provide you with opportunities to advance the sale.

As a sales professional, you need to understand that a customer without an objection is not a customer at all. In fact, raising an objection means the customer is actually engaged in the purchase process.

And that means you're still in the game!

This simple mindset shift will transform the way you look at sales objections. Rather than experiencing the objection as an obstacle, you can now view it as an opportunity.

It means your customer is interacting in the sales process, not impeding it.

This is just one of several strategic mindset shifts I'll present that will make you an expert at handling sales objections.

I guarantee that if you embrace these eight self-study lessons, you will find that objections become your ally— an important asset you can leverage in a positive way to help your customer make a satisfying purchase decision.

And if you've got that sinking feeling in your stomach right now, then pop open the Tums and let's get started. I promise it's not nearly as scary as you think it is!

Handling Sales Objections:
Embrace the Objection

CHAPTER 1

2   HANDLING SALES OBJECTIONS

CHAPTER 1:

Embrace the Objection

I've been in the sales world a long time. The thing I enjoy most is working with salespeople like you on how to advance the sales process and how to help your customers accomplish their purchase objectives.

To do that, you must become adept at handling sales objections.

Perhaps when you think about objections, you have an initial gut reaction: "Oh, no!!! An objection…" I want to suggest that carrying this mindset will get you into trouble right from the beginning.

Instead, I'm going to talk about adopting mindsets and attitudes that will prepare you not just to deal with sales objections but to actually embrace them.

I want to start with mindset because it's particularly critical to this process. Your mindset dictates your strategy.

Bad Mindset = Bad Strategy

By nature, you, like all people, are likely to have a negative response when you hear an objection from a customer. That means you're probably not going to serve his needs as well as you can, and you are most certainly not going to advance that sale.

Let's start by looking at what goes on inside your own mind when you encounter an objection.

Suppose you are deep into the purchase process. You've been working with these people for a while. They like you and you like them. It's all good.

Out of nowhere they raise an objection—and it's a particularly difficult issue. It might have to do with the price, the terms, or something about the product...whatever. The question you need to ask yourself is this: *"What is the most obvious observation I can make about my customer?"*

The most obvious observation you can make is that *the customer is still standing there!*

If the objection were a deal-killer, you would no longer be talking with that customer.

Customers, by nature, don't look at this situation and say, "Hey, you know what? Let me lay out all of the reasons why I'm not gonna buy before I walk out the door forever." That's not typical buyer behavior.

When a customer finds a deal-killing objection, he tends to leave. He's just gone!

If the customer is still there, by extension, it means he is still interested in buying. By raising the objection in the first place, you need to understand that this customer is actually telling you, "Help me!"

EMBRACE THE OBJECTION   5

When you hear an objection, you need to *embrace it*.

You need to recognize that the objection is ultimately a request from the customer for help. The customer has a legitimate issue and he simply does not have a satisfying answer to help him deal with that concern. This is where you come to the rescue.

If you get this mindset right, suddenly everything changes.

If you think of an objection as a negative, then you're likely to go into a defensive mental mode against your customer. You're going to play the "is so… is not…" game. That's not what you want to do.

If you see raising objections as your customer saying "help me," you're not going to be argumentative. You're going to become an *advisor* to him, a partner with him. *TOGETHER* you are going to work through this, all in the customer's best interest.

What it comes down to is this: *A real objection indicates a real buyer.* Show me a buyer without an objection and I'll show you a non-buyer.

You need to recognize that objections are *normal*, objections are *natural*, objections are "expected," and objections are, most importantly, a *plea* for help.

If you do, you'll be in a position to become your customer's "hero" by helping him move past his objection and toward the purchase he truly wants to make.

6   HANDLING SALES OBJECTIONS

SELF-STUDY QUESTIONS:

1. *If bad mindset leads to bad strategy, how does good mindset lead to good strategy?* focusing on a positive allows me

2. *Think of an example of a time you helped a customer overcome an objection. How did that feel? Compare that to the feeling you had when you dropped your price without addressing the objection. Which felt better for you? Which felt better for the customer?*

3. *How does dealing with objections as opportunities create a win-win situation for both you and the customer?*

4. *When was the last time you felt like a hero as a salesperson in the eyes of the customer?*

EMBRACE THE OBJECTION

Handling Sales Objections:
The Reality of Compromise

CHAPTER 2

10   HANDLING SALES OBJECTIONS

CHAPTER 2:

The Reality of Compromise

In Chapter 1, we talked about the idea that a customer's objections are natural and normal. In fact, they are the customer's way of saying, "Can you help me with this issue?"

We should be thankful that the customer is voicing the objection.

She is offering you something of a gift, the opportunity to help and serve. Offer your gratitude in return. *"Thanks for sharing your concerns. I can actually help you more when I know what you don't like, than what you do like."*

Before moving on to discover how you might handle sales objections, you need to understand what causes an objection in the first place.

To do this, you must think like a buyer.

A customer has high hopes and dreams when she begins her search. She has in mind an ideal—everybody wants perfection—the perfect product and the perfect solution. And this leads to a fundamental problem. *Perfection does not exist!*

This ideal is what she wants, but then she is confronted with her perception of what you actually have to offer. Therein lies the conflict. The customer has the ideal on the one hand and her perception of what you are offering on the other.

In the gap between her ideal and her perception lies her objection.

Pretend you are a customer for a moment. You start your search knowing exactly what you want, but what you're finding is *not exactly what you want*. That's where the objection comes into play.

Think about the last car you purchased. You probably had some idea of what you were looking for and what you wanted to spend. If you're like most people, you probably had to make some adjustments.

For example, you wanted the air-conditioned seats and the bird's-eye view camera, but you really didn't want to spend another thousand dollars to get them. There is the objection: the ideal (the features you want) versus the offering (having to pay a lot to get them).

Here's the good news. It does not mean, by any means, that the sale is over.

Objections are the customer's way of saying, "Can you help me with this issue?"

What it means is that you must help your customer understand what compromise(s) she is willing to make. What will it take to satisfy her?

Every customer goes through this process of finding her acceptable level of dissatisfaction.

THE REALITY OF COMPROMISE   13

I wouldn't suggest you use that language in your sales presentation, of course. Just realize that as human beings this is a normal part of the purchase process.

Customers need to face the fact that they're not going to see (or get) perfection!

You want to do all in your power to move your customer away from a perfect ideal. You're not trying to find the perfect solution. You're trying to find the *right* solution. You're trying to find the *best* solution. And I think it's okay to share that concept with your customer.

When she brings up an objection you simply cannot eliminate, you need to communicate with her from the mindset that perfect does not exist. Tactfully, you help her see that she will never find the perfect offering. You can, however, help her to find the *best* choice, the *right* choice. And assure her that you will walk with her through this process until she finds that best, right choice.

Previously, you learned about adopting the right mindset when a customer raises an objection in the first place. Now consider the proper mindset as you attempt to guide your customer through the process of compromise: finding the best possible purchase solution for her.

Point her to the best solution…to the right solution…because there is no perfect solution. That will put you on track to ultimately satisfying your customer—and making the sale.

SELF-STUDY QUESTIONS:

1. *Remember one of the basic bits of advice for customer service folks responding to complaints: Smile, even over the phone. How does thinking of the objection as a gift rather than something negative help you to keep a frown off your face and shift your mindset from bad to good?*

2. *People deal with situations in life where they strive for "good" and "best" rather than "ideal" every day and are quite happy with the results. What are some of these situations in your life?*

3. *How can you help a customer understand that accepting something less than perfection is not only acceptable but good?*

THE REALITY OF COMPROMISE

16   HANDLING SALES OBJECTIONS

Handling Sales Objections:
Three Reality-Embracing Questions

CHAPTER 3

18   HANDLING SALES OBJECTIONS

CHAPTER 3:

Three Reality-Embracing Questions

UNDERSTANDING THE HIERARCHY OF VALUES

A major part of any significant purchase decision falls under the category of "embracing reality."

If you watch House Hunters on HGTV you'll note that every episode starts basically the same way: *"Jack and Barbara and their six kids have outgrown their two-bedroom apartment. Jack and Barbara are looking for a five-bedroom home with three acres that's just a short walk away from the beach and in their price range of $180,000."*

Now, if you know anything about the show, you also know that whatever Jack and Barbara describe at the beginning of the show is nothing like what they buy at the end! That's because when customers are in the process of buying (and this is particularly true with major purchases), they eventually have to embrace reality.

The Rolling Stones put it this way: "You can't always get what you want."

And you can't!

What's "important" is not what matters; it's what matters most.

Going through the process of embracing reality helps your customer define what really matters most. As a sales professional, one of the most important things you can do for your customer is help him identify his own hierarchy of values. What is truly important and where does it fall in his continuum of value?

What's "important" is not what matters; it's what matters most.

Your job is to help your customer prioritize what matters the most, and then find the solution that checks enough of those boxes. You are helping him purchase in alignment with his hierarchy of values.

I suggest you ask your customer three questions to help him determine what really matters to him. And I mean it...really...start asking your customers these questions!

REALITY-EMBRACING QUESTION #1:

"Is this a 'must-have' or is this a 'really-want-to-have'?"

Many sales trainers will tell you to ask something like, "Is this a 'must-have'?"

But, frankly, I think that's inadequate.

You see, you've got to go one step beyond. You need to ask your customer to identify whether it's a "'must-have" or if it's a "really-want-to-have."

This allows your customer the freedom to acknowledge both to himself and to you, "Listen, I can't say it's a must-have, but I really want to have it!"

Which is fair for everyone! The customer might be passionate about that feature. And if you can give it to him, that's great.

But dealing up front with this question helps to determine two distinct categories in the customer's mind:

1. This is a deal-killer

2. This is *not* a deal-killer

Here's the idea. If it's a "must-have" and you can't give it to him, then he's not going to buy. Period. No sale. Have a nice day.

But if it's a "really-want-to-have" and you can't give it to him, he still might buy if everything else is right.

REALITY-EMBRACING QUESTION #2:

"What do you have now that you really can't live without?"

It doesn't matter what you are selling. Every customer, when he's looking forward to what he's moving to, starts with a paradigm of what he is coming from.

As a buyer thinks about what he's going to buy in the future, his paradigm will be based on what he has bought in the past. And so, as a salesperson, it makes sense to ask the question, "What do you have now that you can't live without?"

This will help you identify not only what he already has, but also why it's important to him. And when you do that, you can move forward with the sales process.

REALITY-EMBRACING QUESTION #3:

"If everything is right, except for this one thing, would you still be interested?"

The idea here is that you're trying to isolate the one issue you can't overcome and remove it from the purchase decision.

What you're asking your customer to do is make a balanced decision. You're framing the purchase decision in a more realistic manner.

Let's finish where we started. Do you remember how the Rolling Stones continue that line from their song?

"You can't always get what you want. But if you try sometimes, you just might find, you get what you need."

Your customer can't always get what he wants. But if you help him identify what he needs, you are well on your way to creating one more happy buyer!

SELF-STUDY QUESTIONS:

1. *How does helping a customer distinguish between "must-have" and "really-want-to-have" help you become a hero for that customer?*

2. *Every customer starts with a perspective of what he is coming from (current situation). Thinking about that, why is it important to find out what your customer loves about his current situation (or product)?*

3. *Think about the concept, "you can't always get what you want." What could you do to influence your customer to overcome their objection to the "one thing" that is holding him back from moving forward with the purchase?*

24 HANDLING SALES OBJECTIONS

Handling Sales Objections:
The Law of Social Proof

CHAPTER 4

26   HANDLING SALES OBJECTIONS

CHAPTER 4:

The Law of Social Proof

As a regular part of any sales training, any sales meeting, and likely any sales coaching session, sales professionals are instructed on how to deal with common objections. You've likely been handed a script at some point and told, "Here. Memorize this."

Furthermore, you have probably bounced ideas off your peers and listened to the way that they have handled such difficult situations. We've all "borrowed" some of the better lines that make their way into our sales presentation, right?

Finally, I'm going on the assumption that you have read my book *Deal With It!* (available on Amazon.com!) and memorized specific passages, right? RIGHT?

Okay, all good. You want to be prepared. Good job. When your customer is raising an objection, you can certainly share your opinion.

But…wouldn't it be so much better if you could *share the opinion of someone who has already decided to buy?*

Let's face it: other customers have traveled this path already. They had these same objections…and they bought anyway. There has to be some way to use their stories.

28   HANDLING SALES OBJECTIONS

This is what the venerated psychologist Robert Cialdini refers to as the "Principle of Social Proof." In short, *people are inclined to do what people like them are inclined to do.*

It's one thing to try and deal with an objection yourself, but it's completely different if you bring in the story of someone who has had to deal with that same issue and ended up creating her own solution to the problem.

At some point in your sales career you have likely been taught a technique known as "feel, felt, found." It goes something like this. "I know how you *feel*. Others have *felt* the same way. But they *found* that…"

Let's dissect that, beginning with the start of the technique.

"I know how you *feel*…" STOP RIGHT THERE! If your customer raises an objection and you immediately respond with "I know how you feel…" you risk losing credibility. Here's why: You're the *salesperson*, not the buyer.

You could have a customer thinking, "Do you? Do you really know how I feel? Do you have to make this decision? Do you have to live with the compromise? Oh, and by the way, do you get paid when I decide to purchase?"

She is not going to say this, of course. It might not even be in the forefront of her mind. But it definitely can raise a red flag.

Try this instead: *"I have an opinion on that, but I'm also not walking in your shoes here. So let me tell you how other people have dealt with this issue. Their opinions matter more than mine."*

THE LAW OF SOCIAL PROOF   29

People are inclined to do
what people like them are inclined to do.

I'm now taking it out of my perspective as a salesperson and putting it into the perspective of somebody who actually had to write the check or hand over her credit card. That makes a profound difference.

Use the principle of social proof. Collect the stories of people who have gone before your customer, have made the move, and are now extremely happy they did so.

Again, *people are inclined to do what people like them are inclined to do.* So, leverage the experiences of others to help your customers overcome their objections. Social proof is a powerful principle that can help you help your customer move past her objection and toward a satisfying purchase.

SELF-STUDY QUESTIONS:

1. *Think about a common objection you hear. Now, think back to your most recent successful sale and list three elements of social proof from that customer's perspective.*

2. *Think about a time that you shared your opinion with a customer in an attempt to help her overcome an objection. How could you have handled the situation differently? Looking back, what would you say now?*

3. *List 3 common objections you hear. Then for each objection think of a similar situation with a previous customer, and write out how that customer handled the objection.*

THE LAW OF SOCIAL PROOF   31

32   HANDLING SALES OBJECTIONS

Handling Sales Objections:
Transfer of Ownership

34   HANDLING SALES OBJECTIONS

CHAPTER 5:

Transfer of Ownership

If you have any history in sales, you've probably built up a small reference library of answers to sales objections that you frequently face.

The customer complains about this...I'm going to respond with that. The customer raises an objection here...I've got my answer over there.

Top performers feel prepared for most of these situations.

That said, there are times in the sales process where you will find yourself completely stumped by a particularly difficult objection. You'll suddenly find yourself in a situation where you simply have no clue how to respond.

For example, I once had a customer tell me that the home I was trying to sell him was haunted.

I had no answer for that issue.

If you've got an answer for that, I'm all ears...Please email me at jeff@jeffshore.com

But seriously, as much as we all want to load up a silver bullet for

36   HANDLING SALES OBJECTIONS

every objection…that's just not realistic.

However, think this through for just a moment from the customer's perspective. The customer is already involved in this process. He's sharing the objection because he is interested. Remember, if he had eliminated this option because of a deal-killing issue, he would not be talking to you—he would be out the door.

Any time you offer a solution to an objection, you are asking the customer to adopt your perspective. What difference do you think it would make if the customer came up with the answer to his objection *himself?*

If the customer comes up with his own solution, how much stronger do you think that solution will be in the customer's mind?

We call this the "transfer of ownership" technique. This occurs where we transfer ownership of the solution back to the customer.

In this situation, I ask questions like these:

- *"What would you do if you already owned it?"*

- *"If you had to come up with a solution, how would you solve this issue?"*

- *"What would you do if this was the only _____ available to you?"*

TRANSFER OF OWNERSHIP   37

What I'm asking the customer to do is to *solve his own problem.*

Here's the beautiful part of this. If the customer comes up with his own solution, how much stronger do you think that solution will be in the customer's mind?

If the customer comes up with the solution himself, that solution is now coming from within. And people don't tend to argue with themselves. At that point, they are *much more likely to buy into the solution.*

I want to encourage you to play around with this idea of the transfer of ownership. How can you take that objection and put it back on the shoulders of your customer?

It's an advanced technique, but I'm telling you, once the customer comes up with the solution, that objection will be done, done, done!

And once that objection is gone, you're one step closer to closing the sale!

SELF-STUDY QUESTIONS:

1. *Think about a common objection you hear. Using that objection, come up with 2-3 questions you could ask your customer to transfer the ownership of the solution back to him.*

2. *If a customer is hesitant to come up with his own solution to an objection, how can you work with your customer to persuade him to identify the solution? What might you suggest, and why?*

3. *How would or should you react when the customer comes up with his own solution?*

TRANSFER OF OWNERSHIP

40   HANDLING SALES OBJECTIONS

Handling Sales Objections:
Can You Live With It?

CHAPTER 6

42   HANDLING SALES OBJECTIONS

CHAPTER 6:

Can You Live With It?

At the beginning of this book, we talked about adopting a right mindset, a mindset that embraces objections and views them as a plea for help.

If we choose this approach, we can say to our customers, *"I want to help you look at that objection, because I want to help you find the best solution. Not the perfect solution—because that probably doesn't exist—but the right solution for you."*

We all know there are times when our customers will come to us with an objection that, no matter what we do, simply can't be overcome. There is a word for that situation: "normal."

It happens all the time, because there's no such thing as perfect. Yet, that is certainly what some customers are looking for.

It is not your job as a salesperson to find the perfect solution.

Your job is to help the customer find the best solution.

44 HANDLING SALES OBJECTIONS

So, part of your job is to help your customers understand that perfect doesn't exist, and guide them toward determining their acceptable level of dissatisfaction. We need to lead them in the discovery of their own hierarchy of values, to figure out what really matters to them.

For example, there was something I wanted in the last car I purchased: air-conditioned seats. Yes, that's a thing. You can make the seat cool on a hot day. And why did I want this particular feature? Simple: because my wife has it in her car.

I told the dealer the list of features that I wanted in the new car. He got close, really close. He basically showed me a car with everything I wanted, except for…you guessed it…air-conditioned seats.

He could see that I was disappointed but he also knew that this particular vehicle would be as close to perfect as we were going to get. He asked the question: *"Since everything else is just what you're looking for, and you're not going to get closer to your wish list than this, can you give up the air-conditioned seats?"*

You probably can guess what I did. I bought the dang car! And now several years later I rarely think about that feature (well, except, of course when I think to use it as a sales training example like this!).

The technique is called: Can you live with it?

There are times you're going to have to look at the customer and say, *"If everything else is right, can you still enjoy this the way it is?"*

What you are doing for the customer is helping her to separate the "really-wants" from the "must-haves." If the customer cannot live with the solution, that means it is absolutely a deal-killer.

Which means that:

1. It's not a sale.

2. She's outta there.

But if the customer chooses to stay, then the answer to the question, *"Can you live with it?"* is typically…"yes."

She may only be 90% thrilled with it now. But she's still pretty thrilled. And she may very well still buy because, overall, the trade-offs involved are worth it.

So, here's the ten-million-dollar question for your customer, *"If everything else works for you, is this something that you can live with?"*

Ask it calmly and confidently, letting the customer know that there is no such thing as perfect.

And remember, it is not your job as a salesperson to find the perfect solution. Your job is to help the customer find the *best* solution.

And when you do, you'll be on the home stretch in the sales process.

SELF-STUDY QUESTIONS:

1. *Why is it better to ask "If everything else is right...?" than to ask "If this is the only thing wrong...?"*

2. *How could you use the car sale example in this chapter to get a customer to recognize that there is never a "perfect" solution?*

3. *What will you do if you ask "Can you live with it?" and the customer says "No," but doesn't exit the sales conversation? Is there still hope of a sale or are you wasting time?*

4. *Think of a time when you were dealing with a customer who was "picky." She couldn't seem to commit to a purchase, because no matter how hard you tried she had some objection to the product. What would you have done differently in the scenario to convince her that perfect doesn't exist and guide her toward determining her acceptable level of dissatisfaction?*

CAN YOU LIVE WITH IT? 47

48   HANDLING SALES OBJECTIONS

Handling Sales Objections:
He Likes It...
She Doesn't

CHAPTER 7

50 HANDLING SALES OBJECTIONS

CHAPTER 7:

He Likes It... She Doesn't

CONFLICTED CO-BUYERS

What do you do when one buyer likes what you're selling, but the co-buyer does not?

She wants blue; he wants green. He wants large; she wants small. You get the picture.

The bottom line? If you've got more than one decision-maker, you've got a challenge.

In sales training, we tend to look at the process as involving one salesperson and one customer. And yet, we all know that this is often not the case.

Whether it's a husband and wife buying something together, two business partners making a company purchase, parents and children, or any transaction involving more than one person, the sales process becomes more complex. It will involve more than one decision-maker.

So, now you're dealing with more than one decision-making style.

But, more importantly, you're now dealing with more than one set of values.

The placid river ride suddenly hits the white water rapids!

So, let's agree that it's significantly easier if you are selling to one person and having a one-on-one conversation. But, if you have multiple decision-makers, you need to approach the sale in a new way.

You must consider the question, *"What do I do if one likes it and the other doesn't?"*

Let's suppose you are selling to a husband and wife and he likes it but she doesn't, or vice versa. What do you do? In any relationship, who wins? Let me give you a clue…

I travel a lot. When I get home on the weekend I might say something like, "Hey, Karen, you want to just go out for dinner tonight?"

So she says, "Sure…you want to go up to Maria's? I could go for their Caribbean chicken salad."

At that point, I might look back at her and say, "If that's what you really want, babe, then I could do that. But I gotta tell you…I've been jonesin' really bad for Mikuni's. I want sushi so bad! So…can we please, please, please go to Mikuni's?"

Do you know what she's most likely going to say next? "Sure…we can go to Maria's next time."

And then we'll go to Mikuni's.

Now, why did I "win" that argument?

Not because of my persuasive abilities and not because of the nature of our relationship. The fact is that it could have gone the other way.

I could have started by saying, "Hey babe, do you want to go out to Mikuni's tonight?"

To which she could have responded, "Umm...not really. Can we do Maria's instead? *I've been dying* for their Caribbean chicken salad. It sounds soooo good right now. Can we *please go to Maria's?!*"

And, guess what? In that moment, there's a good chance my answer would be, "Sure, let's do it."

So, what's really going on here? How is this conversation being swayed?

The answer comes in the form of an intriguing psychological phenomenon: the passion always wins!

In a dispute between a buyer and a co-buyer, your job is to *follow the passion.*

In fact, you need to follow the passion trends throughout the entire buying process.

What you'll discover is that one person may be more passionate here, and the other more passionate there. Follow the passion and you'll see where the decision is headed.

Follow the passion!
The passion always wins.

This can leave you with a difficult question though.

In a tense standoff, how do you make it easy for the passionate person to win without making the other party feel like a loser?

There is a simple technique for that.

When you find yourself in this situation, you can ask this question of the less passionate person: *"Is this something you're willing to compromise on so that you can make _____ happy?"*

What are you doing? You're taking the person who is less passionate and *making him or her the hero.*

I believe the more passionate person is going to win the argument anyway. But now I've made the less passionate person the "good guy," the hero of the story.

This is a win-win strategy that allows both parties to feel good about the end result.

And, guess what? When you're successful, you become a hero, too!

SELF-STUDY QUESTIONS:

1. *You're not a relationship counselor. How is "following the passion" different from giving relationship advice?*

2. *How do you "follow the passion" if neither decision-maker sounds particularly passionate? How can you work to uncover stronger emotions?*

3. *Why would the "follow the passion" approach work better when asking for a sale, then asking the two decision-makers to revisit their lists of wants, needs and objections?*

4. *Think about a time you have dealt with two decision-makers during the sales process. What indicators did you see that made it apparent that one individual was more passionate about the product? How could you use these indicators to sway the less passionate individual?*

56   HANDLING SALES OBJECTIONS

Handling Sales Objections:
We Need To Think About It

CHAPTER 8

58 HANDLING SALES OBJECTIONS

CHAPTER 8:

We Need To Think About It

Let's wrap this up by addressing the granddaddy objection of them all: "We need to think about it."

I don't care what you're selling. I don't care how long you've been selling. I don't care what your style is. I don't care what your product is. It doesn't matter. Somewhere along the line you're going to hear the most common objection in the sales world: "We need to think about it."

This is going to happen; you need to be prepared for it.

Alas, all too often this is a sale-stopping moment. The customer offers the think-about-it objection, and the salesperson basically throws in the towel.

Part of the problem lies in the fact that you've probably not been well prepared to handle this particular issue. Perhaps you've been in a sales training session where a trainer gives you an auto-response that goes something like this…

Customer: *"We need to think about it."*
Salesperson: *"Well, what do you need to think about?"*

Do you hear the potentially combative tone in that retort? It's as if

60   HANDLING SALES OBJECTIONS

the salesperson is demanding an answer.

Here's another problem. Sometimes, when a customer says, "I want to think about it," you might decide that this is code language that is covering up her real message.

You immediately begin to think that there must be something she is not telling you. There must be a stirring issue that you have not yet uncovered.

Here's a different take: perhaps she really does want to think about it.

Seriously, some people need time to process.

If you confront her as to what specifically she wants to think about, you'll likely back her into a corner. The mental dialogue in response to the challenge will sound something like this:

"Well, I don't know what I need to think about. So, I guess I need to think about what I need to think about. After I think about that, then I'll think about whether I'm going to call you again."

Allow me to make a couple of suggestions that might be more helpful.

First, if your customer says she needs to think about it, it means she probably hasn't been given the chance to clarify her thoughts along the way.

It is your job as a sales professional to help the customer make a series of small agreements throughout the buying process. I recommend asking clarifying questions like:

WE NEED TO THINK ABOUT IT   61

- *"Do you like this?"*

- *"Does this work for you?"*

- *"Is that what you were hoping to find?"*

When the customer makes these small agreements along the way, she is constructing an eventual "end-of-the-process" decision in her mind. The customer is making active, conscious decisions, and this moves her along in the buying cycle.

If you are not asking those small questions, is the customer still making decisions? She most certainly is, but they are non-conscious decisions. They are not active decisions, and that makes them harder to process mentally and emotionally when asked for a decision.

In such instances—when you finally ask the customer to purchase—she needs to go all the way back through her mind to try and assimilate her entire series of non-conscious decisions. And this is really hard to do!

If you're hearing "I want to think about it" from your customers on a regular basis, I challenge you to go back and consider how frequently you asked them to make those little agreements throughout the sales process.

It is your job as a sales professional to help the customer make a series of small agreements throughout the buying process.

62   HANDLING SALES OBJECTIONS

This approach of small "yeses" along the way establishes a decision-making rhythm. It helps your customer get into a mindset that says, "Yes, I do like that." "That does work for me." "That is the right choice." She is in a "yes" type of mood.

Here's the good news. If she has already said, "Yes," to these smaller decisions, guess what happens next?

This consistent decision-making rhythm creates clarity in making a final purchase commitment.

Let me now revisit the original issue. I suggest that when the customer says, "I want to think about it," you need to take the role of counselor. You need to come alongside her with a statement like, *"I get it. I understand. My job here is to help you in any way that I can to accomplish your goal. So is there any one issue that's really standing out?"*

That's a very different question than, "What do you need to think about?"

"What do you need to think about?" is a brain-frying question. There are a thousand things your customer thinks about. What you need to know is: *What's the biggie?* Is there one thing that is really standing out?

If she is holding back because of one issue—price, timing, relational conflict, whatever—that is what you need to address.

To keep the sale alive, you need to isolate this "biggie" objection, tackle it head on, and get the sales process back on track.

So, the question is not, "What do you need to think about?"

WE NEED TO THINK ABOUT IT   63

The question is, *"What is the one big issue that stands out in your mind? Is there a particular concern that is holding you up?"*

Suppose the customer responds by saying, "No, there's not. There's just too much information to assimilate. I'm a little overwhelmed right now. I just need a little bit of time."

At that point, you're going to have to make the call. That customer may simply not be ready to purchase at that time.

In that instance, consider doing the customer a favor by putting a time limit on how much time she will take to "think about it."

For example, you might say to the customer, *"I get it. I understand there is much to consider. It's Tuesday afternoon and it's getting late. Why don't we do this? I'll call you tomorrow at lunch time. We can talk then and you can tell me what you've decided to do."*

That suggestion is not intended to be high pressure. The fact is, you're actually doing your customer a favor.

If the customer says she wants to think about it, when do you think that consideration will take place?

I'll tell you when… *immediately!* She's going to start processing her decision very quickly. And the longer she takes to process, the harder it is to reach a conclusion. Long buying cycles typically confuse the customer because of excessive evaluation. The brain locks up over time.

So, give her a timeframe. Tell her, *"Great, I'll call you at noon tomorrow and you can tell me what you've decided."*

As a sales professional, being fully prepared to lead your customer through the sales process not only improves your chances for a sale...it improves your chance to *change your customer's world!*

SELF-STUDY QUESTIONS:

1. *What are your worries when you hear a customer say, "I need to think about it..."? How will this chapter help you overcome those concerns?*

2. *While you are discussing your product with a customer, what are some questions you can ask to ensure you are securing their "little agreements"? How will identifying these agreements help you close the sale?*

3. *Is there ever a time you could/would give the customer a chance to "think about it" without leaving the sales location? How might you handle that?*

4. *If your customer wants to "think about it," what approach should you take to follow up with the customer? Why is it important?*

HANDLING SALES OBJECTIONS

WE NEED TO THINK ABOUT IT

68   HANDLING SALES OBJECTIONS

WE NEED TO THINK ABOUT IT

70   HANDLING SALES OBJECTIONS